The Amazon

Jane Bingham

Raintree

Chicago, Illinois

www.capstonepub.com
Visit our website to find out more information about Heinemann-Raintree books.

To order:
☎ Phone 800-747-4992
💻 Visit www.capstonepub.com to browse our catalog and order online.

© 2013 Raintree
an imprint of Capstone Global Library, LLC
Chicago, Illinois

Edited by Rebecca Rissman, Dan Nunn, and
    Catherine Veitch
Designed by Cynthia Della-Rovere
Leveling by Jeanne Clidas
Picture research by Elizabeth Alexander
Production by Victoria Fitzgerald
Originated by Capstone Global Library
Printed and bound in China by CTPS

16 15 14 13 12
10 9 8 7 6 5 4 3 2 1

Library of Congress Cataloging-in-Publication Data
Bingham, Jane.
  The Amazon / Jane Bingham.—1st ed.
    p. cm.—(Explorer tales)
  Includes bibliographical references and index.
  ISBN 978-1-4109-4780-2 (hb)—ISBN 978-1-4109-4787-1 (pb) 1. Ecology—Amazon River Region—Juvenile literature. 2. Biotic communities—Amazon River Region—Juvenile literature. 3. Amazon River—Juvenile literature. I. Title.
  QH112.B56 2013
  577.09861'6—dc23   2011041467

Acknowledgments
We would like to thank the following for permission to reproduce photographs: Alamy pp. 6 (© Susan E. Degginger), 8 (© North Wind Picture Archives), 9 (© The Art Gallery Collection), 10 (© David Tomlinson), 12 (© Travel Elite Images), 16 (© Pictorial Press Ltd), 21 (© The Art Archive), 27 (© SnapperUK), 28 (© The Print Collector), 29 (© INTERFOTO); Corbis p. 11 (© Bettmann); Dreamstime.com p. 5 (© Jlye); FLPA pp. 18 (© James Christensen/Minden Pictures), 19 (© Michael & Patricia Fogden/Minden Pictures); Getty Images pp. 7 (luoman/Vetta), 22 (Universal History Archive/Hulton Archive), 26 (Fernanda Preto/LatinContent), public domain p. 24; Shutterstock pp. 14 (© JaySi), 20 (© Dr. Morley Read), 25 (© costas anton dumitrescu); TopFoto p. 15 (The Granger Collection).

Cover photographs of Alexander von Humboldt reproduced with permission of Corbis (© Bettmann); section of South America, 1806, Terra Firma, Peru, Brazil reproduced with permission of Sanders of Oxford, rare prints & maps (www.sandersofoxford.com); wooden bungalows, Amazon River, Brazil reproduced with permission of Shutterstock (© JaySi). Interior background photograph of wooden bungalows, Amazon River, Brazil reproduced with permission of Shutterstock (© JaySi).

Contents

Some words are shown in bold, **like this**. You can find out what they mean by looking in the glossary.

The Amazing Amazon

The Amazon rain forest is steamy, dark, and dangerous. It is home to millions of creatures and plants. In the heart of the forest is the Amazon River. It runs more than 3,700 miles across South America.

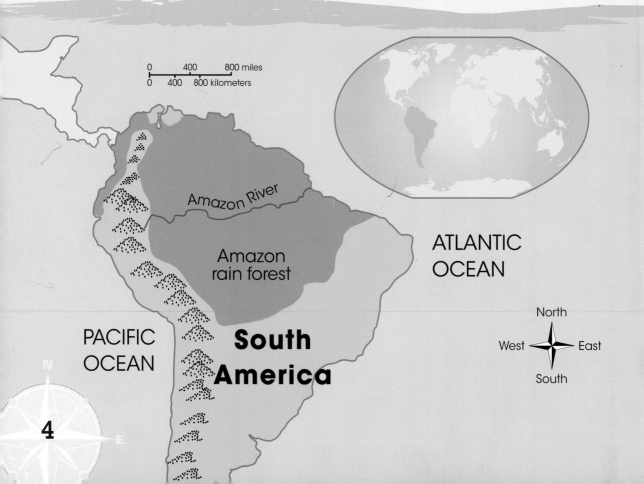

0 400 800 miles
0 400 800 kilometers

Amazon River

Amazon rain forest

ATLANTIC OCEAN

PACIFIC OCEAN

South America

North
West ✦ East
South

DID YOU KNOW?

The Amazon rain forest is so huge it would cover two-thirds of the United States.

jaguar

The rain forest is full of hidden dangers.
Jaguars wait silently, ready to pounce.
Snakes glide through the trees. Deadly
piranha fish swim in the rivers. Piranha
fish can strip the flesh from your bones
in just five minutes!

The native Amazon people know how to survive in the forest. They are expert hunters and farmers.

Searching for Gold

In the 1500s, some brave explorers left Europe. They headed for South America. The explorers had heard stories about a city of gold. The stories said **El Dorado** was ruled by a magical, golden king.

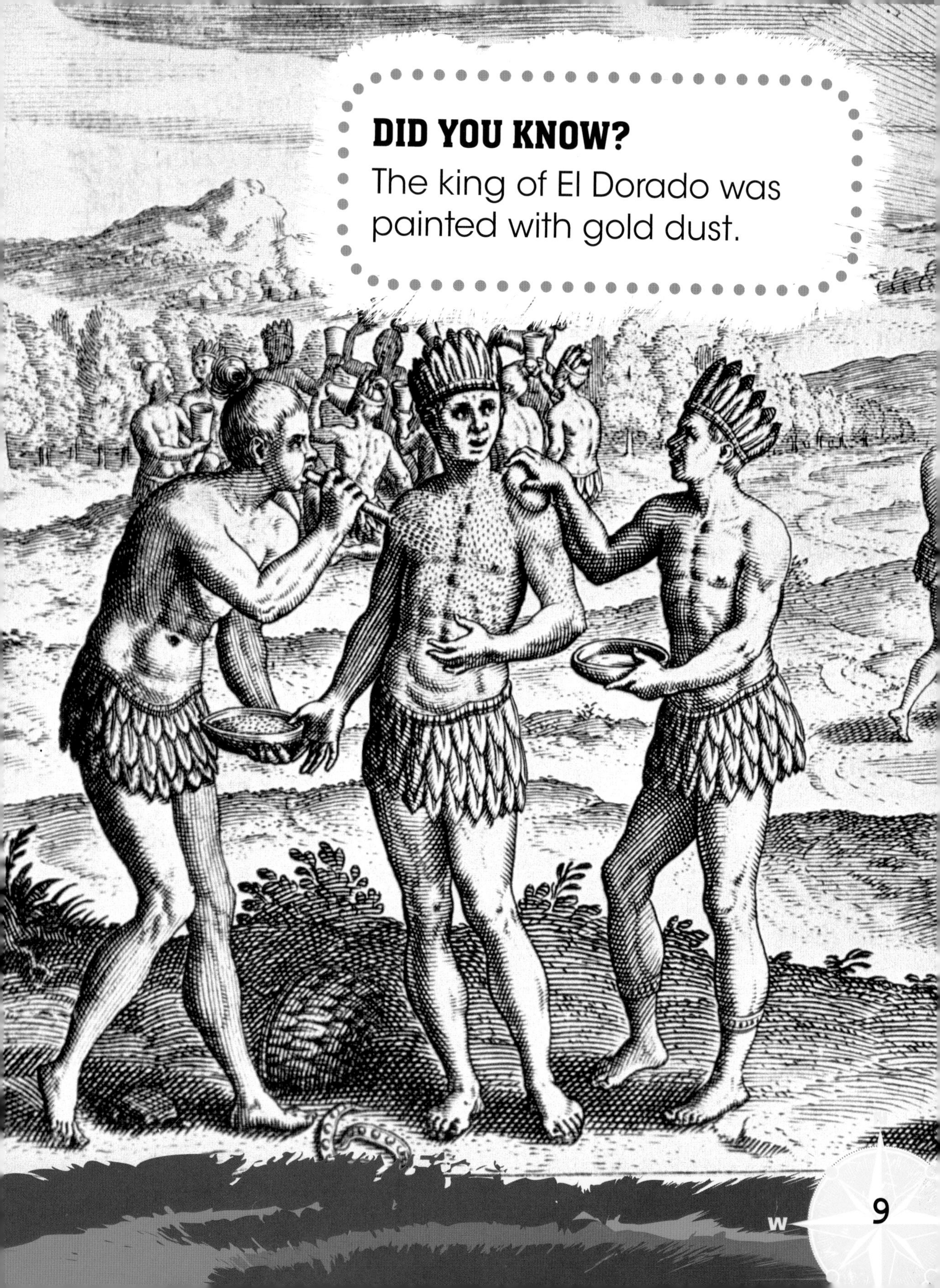

DID YOU KNOW?

The king of El Dorado was painted with gold dust.

First Down the Amazon

Francisco de Orellana was a Spanish explorer. In 1541, he led an **expedition** to search for **El Dorado**. After 10 months, the explorers ran out of food. But Orellana had a plan. He ordered his men to build a boat. Then he set off with 50 men. He promised he would return with food.

Spanish explorers met the local people.

Orellana's boat was carried very fast down the Napo River (see the map on page 13). In August 1542, the explorers reached the Amazon River.

River travel can be very dangerous!

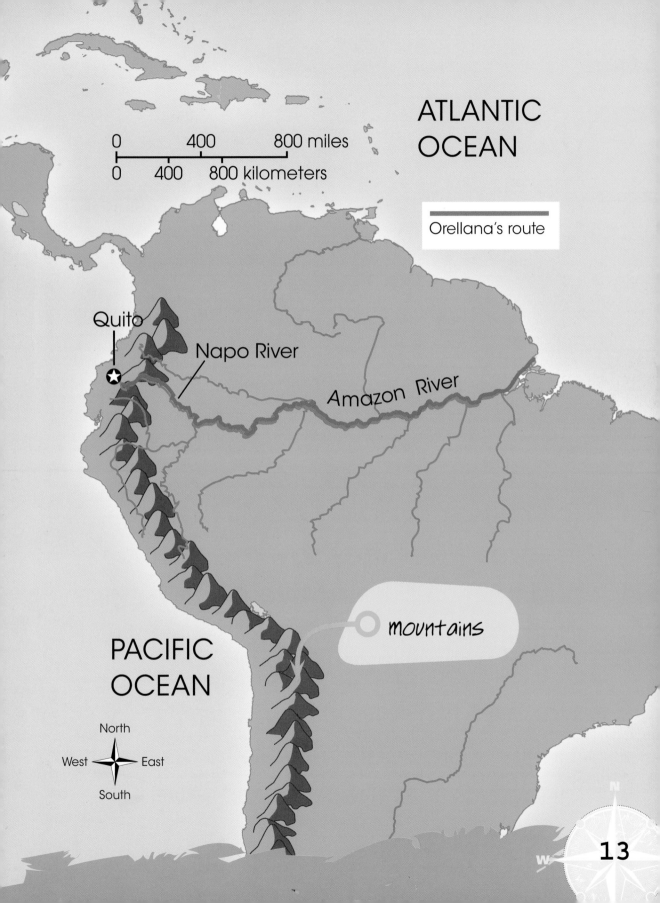

ATLANTIC
OCEAN

0   400   800 miles
0   400   800 kilometers

Orellana's route

Quito

Napo River

Amazon River

PACIFIC
OCEAN

North
West ← → East
South

mountains

13

Most Amazon homes are built on stilts because the river often floods.

The explorers rowed slowly down the Amazon River. They saw many villages and farms. Some **native** people gave them food. Some shot poison arrows at their boat! Finally, the explorers reached the Atlantic Ocean. They were the first European people to travel all the way down the Amazon River.

Orellana and his men would have traveled in a boat like this.

Isabela's Adventure

In 1749, a man named Jean Godin traveled from Riobamba to Cayenne (see the map on page 17). This was a journey of more than 3,000 miles. Jean left his wife, Isabela, behind in Riobamba.

Isabela and Jean lived apart for many years.

Jean thought he would soon return home. But he was not allowed to leave Cayenne. After many years of living alone, Jean sent a boat to Lagunas to wait for Isabela.

Riobamba

Cayenne

ATLANTIC OCEAN

Amazon River

Lagunas

Isabela's route

PACIFIC OCEAN

North

West — East

South

0   400   800 miles
0   400   800 kilometers

Before she could catch the boat, Isabela had to reach Lagunas. In 1769, she set off with 42 people. They crossed the Andes Mountains and **trekked** through the forest. Some of the travelers died from **exhaustion**. Some were attacked by vampire bats. Only Isabela was left alive.

DID YOU KNOW?

Vampire bats can carry a deadly disease called **rabies**.

Isabela **staggered** on through the rain forest. After nine days, she met some **native** people. They took care of her until she was stronger. Then they took her to her boat.

The boat took Isabela all the way down the Amazon River. Then it traveled up the coast to Cayenne. At last Isabela and Jean were together again!

Isabela would have traveled on a boat like this.

The Man Who Loved Birds

Henry Bates was a wildlife expert. In 1848, he went to South America to search for rare creatures. At first he lived in Pará, close to the sea. But he wanted to travel deep into the rain forest. So he set off down the Amazon River.

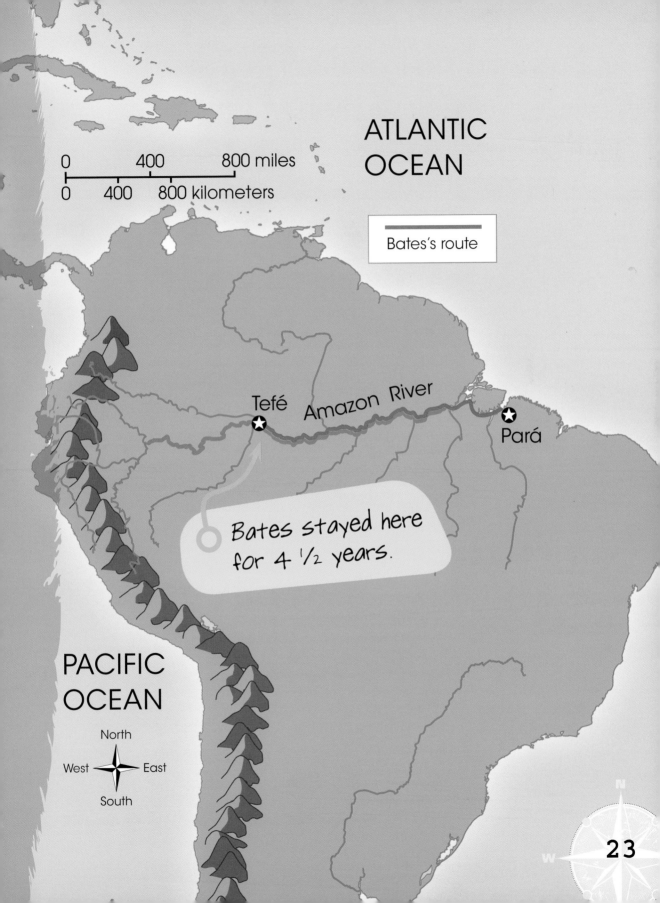

ATLANTIC OCEAN

0   400   800 miles
0   400   800 kilometers

Bates's route

Tefé   Amazon River

Pará

Bates stayed here for 4 ½ years.

PACIFIC OCEAN

North
West — East
South

Bates stayed in the rain forest for 11 years in total. He saw **toucans** with huge, colorful bills. He saw tiny **hummingbirds** and giant spiders. He even saw a spider eating a bird!

DID YOU KNOW?

Bates nursed a sick toucan back to health. The bird became his friend, and they shared all their meals.

Exploring the Amazon Today

People still explore the Amazon today. Explorers search for lost cities. Scientists look for plants. In the 21st century, the Amazon is still a place of mystery and excitement.

Scientists dig for pottery that belonged to people long ago.

DID YOU KNOW?

Plants from the Amazon rain forest are used in medicines for treating many illnesses today.

Timeline

1500s   Explorers from Spain and Portugal start to travel in South America.

1541 – 1542   Francisco Orellana and his crew travel the whole length of the Amazon River.

1769 – 1770   Isabela Godin travels from Riobamba to Cayenne.

1848 – 1859   Henry Bates explores the Amazon rain forest.

Explorers were fascinated by the Amazon and its people.

Glossary

El Dorado magical city rich in gold

exhaustion condition where a person does not have much strength and is too tired to continue onward

expedition long journey to explore a place

hummingbird tiny bird that is the same size as a butterfly

native person born in a particular place. Native Amazon people were born in the Amazon.

rabies very serious disease that usually kills people

stagger walk in a very unsteady way

toucan bird with a large, brightly colored beak

trek walk a very long way, often across rough ground

Find Out More

Books

Callery, Sean. *Rainforest* (Life Cycles). New York: Kingfisher, 2011.

Fitzpatrick, Anne. *Amazon River* (Natural Wonders of the World). Mankato, Minn.: Creative Education, 2005.

Ganeri, Anita. *Living in the Amazon Rain Forest* (World Cultures). Chicago: Raintree, 2008.

Websites

www.nationalgeographic.com/features/00/ earthpulse/rainforest/index_flash-feature.html
Explore the sights and sounds of the rain forest at night.

www.pbs.org/journeyintoamazonia/
Play the game "Amazon Explorer" and discover the forest's secrets.

Index